Forethought

Poems

Daniel Mintie

Livingwell Publishing
Taos, New Mexico

The author gratefully acknowledges the following publications in which poems in *Forethought* first appeared, sometimes in somewhat different form: *The Midwest Quarterly, Blue Mesa Review, Westview, RiverSedge, Stringtown, Byline, Möbius, Illya's Honey.*

Livingwell Publishing
Taos, New Mexico USA
www.livingwellpublishing.com

Forethought: Poems
ISBN 978-1-7328364-8-8 (Print)
ISBN 978-1-7328364-9-5 (ebook)

For Ollie & Brody
bon voyage, mes chers

Forward

The world stands up. The sentence points to something and is itself an instance of this something. The world stands up in the statement. Such is the nature of language, a natural occurrence, rising with the iris in April, the sandhill crane in September.

Written and spoken words stand up first in the mind - thought being another natural occurrence. Early hominids devoted enormous amounts of precious energy to evolving a neocortex, home of human thinking. As a result, mentation has become our species' dominant trait. Most of us, most in the time, live first in a mental topography.

The poems in this book are instances. Each points to a world standing up *before* our thinking, before our saying anything about it to ourselves or anyone else. I hope reading them refreshes your experience of this world, as writing them has refreshed mine.

Contents

The Man Of Great Peace

The man of great peace has no name
for this he is known everywhere

he is the intimate the firstborn
indigene of an indigence

great flower of earth
from which the morning star

steps forth in person
steps forth in this first person

white gold bangle
eye of an ignorant man

first luminary unknown
to any other as to himself

the man of great peace rests in peace
his corpse is our idea of him

Sincerity

We received no marks for it
on our report cards

not even in fourth-year Latin
though its root *sincerus*

meaning *unmixed* comes to us
from the Classical Period

straightforwardness
being like air like sunlight

unnotable save for its effects
this life on earth being

a case in point we're now
beginning to understand

mixes with nothing
not itself without being

cut by that without
bleeding out a little each time

Unconscious
noun (1912)

You entered the lexicon but lately
two years after *curie*
two years before *The Great War*

we having done without you
all that we had done
ably steering the planchette

over the course of millennia
without once looking back in your direction
to see that hand you have in things

accessory dissembled in our bones
as atoms are and armies
and the fugitive reason why

Touché

Vantage point you
little new leaf take

simple inflorescence
lighting the way

shadows alight on this
ground of things

emerald cut on the April air
whetting all senses

single two-edged
blade unsheathing yourself

slaughtering everything
unlike yourself not so

Disambiguation

November wind in the dry leaves
of the cottonwood branches
makes a sound April rain makes
running down the arroyo below

a sound not the sound
of any stream of consciousness
in the middle distance of a middle ear
not the sound of something else

sunder of silk scarves say
fracas of stones in a rain stick
a sound sans precedent or riposte
sounding the singular silence

sole anecdote and history of itself
whole and perfect story
like that cockamamie preaching
from the mouths of babes

Fine Words Butter No Turnips

Nor any tuber speak of this
it's place in the prior ground

from which green sprouts
toplofty per its poems

vert clerestory factories
proclaiming their rootstock

storybooks of the telling
that must leastwise

sustain us in such times
bitter though they be

Incommunicado

In the shadow words make
something is moving

some nameless thing
though called by every name

a thing unspoken
in its saying as its silence

quite like ourselves too close
precisely to be told

that is exactly that
we say not more not less

listen
its sky is sometimes blue

Pupil

Black hole
at the center
of the eye
of a beholder

intimate
of mirrors
o'
of clocks

absence wherein
the whole
earth registers
student of letters

dark kingdom
entered upon
being entered
per you

blind gate
once even
the wildcat
passed through

rippling uncast
shadow single-
minded crouched
inside looking out

Pulse

One stoke of a dead blow hammer
whole of time that
we know

inmost sound seldom heard
our being that
we are

creatures who take comfort
in all we do without
knowing it

our nowadays sluicing through
all told in this and
inasmuch

To Four Wisdom Teeth

Having traveled together this far
the vegetal jungle the sea salt sinew
and venerable age of the grape

traveled as one we five
esprit et corps cinque face of a die cast
one night beneath summer's stars

themselves dispersing *en route*
lighting the way diaspora of things
center refusing to hold

letting go everything
keeping us as headlong we decamp
this place of our arising

farewell hard bits of me
I of thee selves of each other o intimates
workmates come let us make way

Eastern White Pine

Simplicity is becoming
in any individual
as in this

one arrayed in five
slender blue-
green

needles per fascicle
borne aloft in
thin grey-

green bark grown ridged
and ruddy with age
to a conical

crown giving way in time
to whorled asym-
metric limbs

of light straight-grained
wood much prized
in the tall-

ship era for mainmasts
that being the one
upon which

the vessel the crew the voyage
the whole enterprise
depends

Oldest American Elm

Earth standing up
resting now in the shade of itself

indivisible
except we think so

world record
set in concentric rings

shoulder-to-shoulder
in the fragrant dark

uncountable in effect
though we go on

lingering awhile
in these lacy shadows

of the light dry
interlocking grain

counting our days
our nights breathing

in your breathing out
the whole sum

Companionway

*The eye with which I see God is the same
eye with which God sees me.*

Meister Eckhart

This eye looking
this apricot in bloom

this April light
black pit and pivot

of benighted day
these instances

like unto stars
bright cohort

decamped in the all-
embracing solitude

camaraderie that is
any single thing

seen clearly seen
through and through

First Owl

Soft timpanist
down from the mountain
at first frost

perched close
by our bedroom window
woof woofing

from the belly
one slow whole note
shuddering

the still-black
gong morning air
makes through

which the voles
and the field mice run
like tones

the under-
and after tones
they are

Mountain Bluebird

Dearest
blue of all

light taken
wing on wing

straightaway
down the azure

straightaway
high thoroughfare

that is everything
said of it

or sung
in one lilting

downslurred
note heard far

into evening's
middle tinctures

each time
for an instant

precisely this
color of you

On The First Day

God created the bushtit
her quick beak fluted tail

tigereye black center-punched
eye and modest plumage

that unmoved mover
this day created her

inquisitive way about
the male and female hollies

the slight pip she makes
to her flock that moves

lissome as a troupe
through the mind of one

watching of one being
watched kith and kin in this

vision in that kinship always
just now flying up

before tomorrow arrives
and the everything coming after

Hawk

Red-tailed because the sun shines
through because here
we stand

watching this ponderous flapping
climb from the sagebrush
into the dry

sapphire air of a day without
precedent in this life
or the next

winged taloned keen-eyed air foil
gaining height in clean
widening arcs

into everything possible because
the sun shines because
here we stand

Kit And Caboodle

Mister Carson wanted it all

the plains tribes too late
discovered that

buffalo hunter had his sights

set on something
beyond that numerable

ruminant mammal

providing like everything else
all that human beings

ever need to live well

altogether in touch
with what is always right

before our eyes

Docket

Innocent we cry
as though we knew

could know
the beginning

the end
of our kinship

with all those other
people places

things going on
of their own accord

we tell ourselves
entering this plea

on our behalf
as the other half

of the story goes on
everywhere around us untold

Environmental

Environs
that which surrounds
but what

if you then me
if us them
if earth its sky

if sky its stars
each star
its whole night

nothing ever
surrounds the night
moving round

and round
black-a-vised
selfsame

élan
vital as an animal
as blood

engorging the heart
fast core
purlieu that is

the nothing
left over the nothing
left out

where does wreck
of the environment begin
the

Environment

Ancien régime
refracted through this
lean-to

needle's eye
looking out on what is
threading it

rivers distances
seasons every oath
sworn against

this air
that sustains it
forever

pulling into
what we go on calling
the future

as though that
were something else
again

Peace

Beginning

what will we not
make of you

middle

of things goings-on
oh world without

end

Hatred

It's me you love
me alone

as you say *I love
my family my friends*

it's me speaking me alone
saying what you do

me alone who survives
and will

breeding in you my progeny
the world over

o my flame
o inamorato

Complicit

This silence we feed on
feeds upon us

and grows

it must be so
things must be so

we say to ourselves

in the confines of a heart
being nibbled

like the cottage of a witch

who eats young children
and that is a feast day for her

we are told

Fear

I am your best feature
and last faculty

feel me making your way
through everything

you fear not the future
forever closing behind you

your parapets are nothing to me
your reasons your regrets

it's I who take up
your arms your flag

your many points of view
I am what remains

of you I am
your last hope

Karma

This too is the last time
and the next
imperfect shape
of things to come

heretofore
as is seed

progeny-cum-
progenitor of that

preceding-
cum-proceeding

root and bough
flower and fruit

one life
in so many

lifetimes each
touching on

each in this
present perfectly

alive this doing
that has that

is that
will be done

Headlines

Nonevents
going off like failed fireworks
shedding no light

on this occasion
newsworthy in the extreme
unction that is

always the case
whither anyone's looking
say at this first

spring monarch
leaded clerestory wings filtering
morning's amber light

tilting in her tipping
flight the entire balance
in this direction

tidings inseparate
from the moonstruck tides
the ebb and flood

proceeding apace
apprising us of most everything
we'll never know

Dispute Among Parsons

Is it the question that's in error
or the saying so

the redoubt of the visible
neatly hemispheric as a ladybug

lies like a lid on the parish eye
this evening is clear and warm

and beside the point
as heterodox every reason why

new moon
japans a lacquer sky

Self Portrait In Words

What else could there be

these colors too close to call
by any Christian name

these colors and so much else

standing us in place
frame minus reference

things we call *not ourselves*

though night and day
they cry out to us

clearly beseechingly

the first
the given name

Hogback

Any word says more
than can be said

outcropping edge
inclined strata

ascending through
this singular

silence strewn
here at the end

of its long history
in the mouth

of a people who
bite down on

taste are
sustained by that

Silence

Stave
music ascends
resinous
pitch of the pine

timbre of the whole
night wood
riposte
in any tongue

feat
elucidation
preponderant say-
so of stone

displacing speech
testimony
coming before
epitaph

Line

Simplicity

itself running straightaway

silhouette I mean

stream watering figure and ground

near border of the infinite

shortest distance

periphery of what is

of what is not

aperçu of that

difference

saying so

Clean Sheet Of Paper

Note its lines
straight clean and true

the way it altogether
states its case

covers its bases
like darkness like light

like the world itself
write thoroughly

just this once
between the lines

Clef

Now the last birds sing
a cappella in the branches

sing high in the branching
clerestory branches

the leaves are now leaving
wandering off like children

with no idea of arrival
crossing over the river

on a bridge of air
blue-steel openwork

simple truss on which
so much depends

so much that is falling
and calling to be heard

Pronunciamento

Not talk about things
but their saying

December wind's
dry scuttlebutt

a plucked string's
complete report

manufactory
of the whole

corpus brought forth
in earthen notes

fire air and water
plainly speaking

the native tongue
lingua franca completely

explicating this
place of arising

Silence

Surname
of those given after

rhetoric
of things as they are

source
terminus nobody

hears though
some still listen

deer in the woods
Rilke at Duino

those for whom
the saying falls short

as we go on
calling your name

crying out to you
sending you away

Corbeille d'oranges

Matisse in Morocco saw only
what everyone saw

a basket of oranges
setting forth what naught else can

naught else save this
nature morte full-frontal

tipping toward the viewer
proffering itself quietly

as the best things do
terracotta citrus flowering now

against its coral amethyst
and burnt sienna ground

these oranges center the eye
on what sustains us

what we unthinkingly reach for
as a painter his brush

a lover his beloved abed
the African night until sunlight

crashes through the open window
illuminating what had lain hidden

as might some overmastering mind

the rest is rubbish and rind

Mourning Cloak

Asleep on the mountain
through five months of snow

shelved into the sugar pine bark
dreaming or not dreaming

through the nights and days
the ice storms and zeroing wind

a cold that cracks stone
and the skulls of beasts

you reappear this morning
above the footpath by the creek

jet black in full sunlight
as your shadow on clay ground

one-half gram difference
in the way things are

accompanying me awhile
as I do you at shoulder height

place wings affix
in this life in the next

Wild Mustangs

Francisco Vásquez Coronado brought your people
    here
as they carried him and his people
up from New Spain

both peoples having crossed the wide water
via two thousand Iberian oaks
per galleon

that returned to the peninsula bearing another
    people
held as chattel to the crown
as once were you

before escaping with your lives visible now
at sunrise exhaling yellow gold
atop the ridge

Cricket

Selves - goes itself; *myself* it speaks and spells,
Crying *Whát I dó is me: for that I came.*
Gerard Manley Hopkins

Little counselor
heard first at evening
time between

onyx gallant
one half of all you
long to be

soloist
playing at the start
of what is

always falling
petite fiddler dividing night
into equal parts

one coming after
one before desire's bow
troubles its strings

and the whole
arrangement pours out through
the soundboard of you

Sentinel

O do not harm this fly
He wrings his hands
He wrings his feet
　　　Kobayahi Issa

It's taken me this long
to be kind to a fly

one arrived today
on her last legs

at the end of a year
not marked by kindness

clinging to me
as to some last hope

until I lifted her
by one sepia wing

and placed her
feet-first on the window sill

in the weakening sun
of the late afternoon

keeping watch
through her many eyes

Locust

Even your eyes are plated
or look to be

against everything
that isn't so

standing athwart
my garden path

poised in this pale green
spring of yourself

late in the vegetable
wreck of a year

we take in you and I
travel on turn into this

little distance between
the two of us so far

Dearly Departed

You gone but not elsewhere
traveling amazed

as ourselves this
way passing through

road down which
descendant the future

keeps coming to be
the past at no remove

one from another
proceeding altogether

in this one direction
then as now

Adieu Marcel

March 22, 1923 - September 24, 2007

Within this parentheses
days of your coming and going

no text lies

no words set side by side
deriding a life

gestural and beau

the feeling of it lived
largehearted in these limbs

arranged quietly now

in that selfsame stillness
made the more

eloquent their being so

Henri Cartier-Bresson Enters The Light

August 4, 2004

It's what defines us
in the images you made

all the colors of a world
reduced to a single grey scale

in which before our eyes
we become ourselves

becomes most the selves
we are before the looking

o the ceaseless rainbow
looking to see what you see

now your work is done and you
going on into that

Ancientry

Today new thing
stands up in its place

extending outward in all
directions to the far

reaches lit by this
candelabra set high

in the august structure
of the late cottonwoods

tossed implacable light
loud with cicadas

saying what they do
have done and will

Rosette

Exhumed just now
the past creaks into place
over the hill

what's new
we ask trolling Diogenes-
like this dark

water that is
midday without a clue
as to how

we arrive
keep arriving here
the amethyst

bloom
of the lithe desert
willow

our flower
chart compass quick
chronograph

Hit The Mall Whatever

It's later now
not that this helps

clocks were never
friends to whelps like us

keeping busy as elves
emptying the well-

stocked shelves bringing
back everything not

needful in the least
every fixing sans the feast

Requiescat

The past has nowhere to hide
save here in plain sight

manifest carcass
speaking the haruspex' words

reciting in known certain terms
what news we get these days

these nights of errant sally
forth that long last side

Wrist Watch

Nineteen point five
million moments now
you give me this

bracelet inscribed
with all the numbers
called this time

words of love
forever pressed into
a chrome case

reciting what it does
saying everything
it knows of this

present moment
intimate assembly
of so many parts

all working together
at the same time perfectly
like parts of a poem

or any body
of inestimable worth
parsed in these

jeweled movements
bearing us onward together
all at once

Hour Glass

Brilliant
through whose facets
we see

shapeliest figure
upholding the falling
even of stars

silhouette
that is not there
contour

of light
absence air coursing
events

then as now
standing always before us
even in dreams

of falling
from which we awake
just in time

The Good Death

What is it after all
this terminus decampment
manifest station

to which the piñon jays
flock this morning in the pines
note-perfect

in the saying
the compound chorus
chew chewing

this singular
immeasurably curious
mother and lode

good life sprung
structured and struck
at its antipode

Light Dry Alsatian Sun

Things are simpler now
summer's hours settled into place
in these invert sugars

latter-day vintage
of a star we bring to our lips
in deep winter

years from now
inhaling its delicate bouquet
the end of a world

as we know it
December again amongst
the graperies and regrets

Transient

Archfiend old friend
steadfast companion
passer-through
most constant one

amongst the others
soft light emerald verdure
heartwood heat smoke
embers you are

the stalwart
zest of things
lighting the way
awhile like

a comet's tail
we see first
only once
it's gone

Speedboat

Are we there yet
there's nothing new
under the sun

we want there
to be something new
fangled place say

awaiting us
at the end of each day
each night we lay

awake waiting
we know not what how should we
know when it's arrived

Sternwheeler

What goes around
keeps bringing us here

days drenched in azure distance
lacquerware night skies

strewn brightnesses
of one season's return

jasmine-scented
amidst its honeybees

salt in the blood
on its blue circuit

centrifugal traveler
supple *jongleur*

floating two hundred
six bones on the air

Trireme

Past present future
opportune triptych

arriving always
pulling into what-

ever we say of it
as into a port

bearing nothing outside
itself thus laden

far and wide
as every eye can see

Time Flying

Backward against the sun
simple day-cum-night

elided by no movement
of a planet this high

season of velocity in which
the body stunned animal

unable to keep pace
arrives but later

by the clock
on the ground that is

that was that will be
going nowhere at all

Present

What is given
has nothing more

to bequeath
holds nothing back

against any future
itself forever

on complete display
the gift that is

given moment
to moment

like each word
of a prayer

of petition
may I

one day be here
to receive

Four-Quarter

Time beats time on the village clock
and leads the villagers a dance

the clock tower stands
foursquare in the moonlight

its clockwork sprung
its bell bereft of *sprachgefühl*

overhead moon waxes fat on fat
a gibbous moon that old doubloon

waxing hereafter and heretofore
hereinabove hereinbelow

the clock tower standing
stone gnomon at midnight

telling an older colder time
immortal object jocund core

heyday of the villagers' do-si-do
and best and crowning season

History Of The Present Moment

It begins now of course
full issue of itself

phylactery and psalter
of what we say

proceeding horselike
in the horse

prosaic in the prose
of its outright telling

now slicking the bobcat
where she stands

now sleek in the halcyon
motion she rides

down the dry creek bed
at the water's end

Astronomical

The past too we know
is yet to arrive

ladders leaned once
upon a time all the way

to heaven and you
could whole-bodily

climb into the presence
of some preeminent

stained-glass dignitary
indignantly drawing himself

up before your eyes glaring
down at your staring up

heaven's light pouring through
you both at once

illuminating like a manuscript
this darkly brilliant age

In The Beginning

It's like sailing into clearest weather
not separate from the boat
not separate from the material
fact of embarking
setting out not to not from

a stillness manifest as seawater's
unceasing spill as the sea's
overrunning itself green on grey
on its sloping departure
its slant way

If Not For You

Anyone at all
walking ritardando as we do
this bottle-green

world like messages
unthinkingly tucked inside
a day distinguishable

from any other
passing neat-handed by
on a certain street

catching my eye
as did you such that we
read at once

the writ proclaiming
all flesh and blood in this
moment ever since

One For My Dame

My mistress' eyes
are nothing like that

starlight trickles through
dark state of affairs that is

the winter world tonight
nor is her skin to this

black air akin moving
altogether round us as we lie

abed our quiet backwater
of day now done

day unlike any other
comparison being invidious

my dear that is to say
neither there nor here

place we keep finding each other
before ever looking

Tango

Stepping out together as one
into the pure ether that is

Robert Firpo's *Orquesta Típica*
circa nineteen hundred thirty-one

twin bandoneónes sighing
such a thing is possible

either side the grave
we can't know what we do

or don't that makes it so
we know only that

as the music ends the world
returns like a passport

stamped with each profligate
place we've never been

Wire

How is it that copper learned
to speak in your voice

saying the words you say
declaring the colors of your day

recounting the passing hours
as if it knew them in person

alive to that difference one
makes amongst others

I hold this slender strand
of earth to my ear

as I have one of its shells
many miles from the sea

hearing my own heart
speak back the news

Sound Of One Voice

Alone in the comings and goings
I listened not knowing for what

as a wineglass upholds its emptiness
through the long season of the grape

for years in the silence between
words I listened not hearing

what now rises daily about me
overbrimming splashing

brightly to the floor a lifetime's
good fortune handfuls of silver

coin buying back everything
I'd deemed forever lost

Unauthorized Scallion

Such greenery after all
the warships the warstle the wrangling
right and wrong

piquant upstart
standing up in early March
raw opportunist

dew-clad rapier
assailant of status quos
emerald freshet

like any possibility
inordinately slim rising through
the broken concrete

the broken teeth
cynicism scorn received opinion
disclosing what is

forever prior
pointing the way forward
should we care to see

Hobo Jungle

The pieces keep fitting
together elsewise each time
so like this planet

or any other so like
a genus of time now past
commemorated

in this tramp-
art piece from the Thirties
decoupage built

like any from a world
at hand in which nothing is
discarded nothing

conserved plainly
visible right out to the edge
of almost any town

Losing Virginity

Fire is eros I've been
given to understand

these light years
just now sluicing down

through everything
we say of them

everything we do
and fail to do

arising from this
deep sky whose

progeny we are
so straightaway

recognize this first
time as the best

Innocence

Disillusion too will pass
disperse like November ground fog
in morning sunlight

the going of a sudden
become easier as when a bicyclist
drops a gear and the hill-

like disenchantment
gives way to the desenchanter
robed capacious blue

welcoming us arms
outstretched home children
of credence and light

Fleur De Coin

All afternoon
arrives just this way

its colors struck
its sky pewter grey

this afternoon
and every other

struck from
the original die

gilt-edge periphery
silhouette

figure in situ
indefectible ground

flawless specie
uncirculated except at

this still point that is
a turning world

Night

Sight unseen
present absence
nowhere near
wherein we lie

as in our blood
coursing through
its first anatomy
dreamland yes

for all we know
whose stars these are
and will be
as we ourselves

belong less and less
to any other
in these small hours
unlit from above

Beggar

Seated as at table
on this ground that begot you
upholding all morning
the weight of so little in one hand

watching the legs crisscross
on their way elsewhere
hearing the voices quiet and stop
as though approaching

some great mystery
starting again as they move on
like life itself flowing
round you as water round

stone in a stream
diminishing it ever so slightly
freighted now
all the way to the sea

Completely New Direction

Nobody noticed it
or did but didn't
step out until too late

another of the old directions

nobody gave it to anybody else
or did but didn't
realize either of them

or did but didn't

go that way preserving it
terra incognita mare incognitum
abloom like nightfall

black orchid fragrance

scenting the insentience
we must need pass through
wearing like blinders

whatever we know

Ruby-Crowned Kinglet

The pleasure of seeing you
the pleasure of reciting your name
are one pleasure not separate
from the pleasure of saying so

Regulus calendula
petite sovereign of the open-cup nest
olive underparts Egyptian eye ring
clearest edict rung out

on January's air
proclaiming this kingdom
of five senses quintet
through which all

winged thing pass
crowned yes and glorified
by the pleasure of seeing you
the pleasure of reciting your name

Overengineered

So little after all
carried by these cumbrous beams
bearing on practically

anything one might say
about precisely this formwork
scaffolding in which

we find ourselves
strangely silent in the face
of this design we

don't quite fathom
so many redundant systems
of support of aid

and abettance
set round this our endless
falling into place

Singularity

At one point we cease to know
the rules for what happens

next as winter returning to spring
the many returning to what

we call one as though that is
a thing one could call out

like the name of God
that being much too near

to hear us too close
in this life ever to meet

On The Interpretation Of Waking Life

A chair is but a chair
this side of things

stout oaken strut
seat of such knowledge

upon which to depend
to come to rest at this

dimensional compass
of material things

throne for the exegete
Herr Docktor's sedan

aboard which he might travel
so far abroad might finally

plumb the deep blue azimuth
of his extravagant regard

Creation Myth

I think therefore I am.
René Descartes

Herein lies the crux of things
a back-formation self-
evident

as the flatness of the earth
dead level in the eye
and inner ear

great plane the shadows
cross while the fire
rises behind

René *mon frère* behold the ships
weigh anchor and sail
straight away

sinking from sight as day
sinks in the west
each night

thinking is doing that does away
with even the wiliest
things we say

Stevensgraph

It's the unwinged brings it forth
into a light with which it is

interwoven as the rainbow
it depicts as each of these

latter-day mulberry leaves
all their days and nights

clearly visible in this scene
lifted from other lives

radiant now in this one
translucent as eyesight

as the air that little
breezes cross through

Temple Bell

Not past not to come
this singular age called bronze

a long time untold
beneath its mountain

telling now of the efforts
on the part of so many

to bring forth one unseen
note not separate from

April's green air intoning
the passage chapter and verse

song of the songs on this
unalloyed road home

Aircraft
So many parts that cannot fly
as boats are so many

things that disassembled sink
like stones through the lucid

element bearing them up
hearts are born aloft

by everything they're not
air of course as water

knowing as unknowing
hatred as love

oneself as another
this entire present

company flying on
against all the odds

Japan

As it isn't here
I'm going

there too it will not be
the waves the light

the sounds the colors
not be the pines

the cranes flying
from here to here

as I am flying
across earth's face

looking out through
many different eyes

on this one
this only place

Naiveté

From the Latin *nativus*
for native but of what

prior state or place
worldly wise as the raven

eyeing her bright snowfield
this January morning

one so utterly black
taking in unutterable white

as easily as she herself is
taken in embraced by all that

she is not without being
fooled for an instant

Laptop Battery

These words
in their prior state

illegible as yet
potential inseparate from

that silence that steel
that coal that fires

that turning one
thousand miles west

of this place joined by lines
bearing that current first

made visible in these
black runes bespeaking it

traveling on otherwise
neuron-to-neuron

discharging the canticle
body electric deployed in this

far-flung anatomy *full*
with the charge of the soul

Petroglyphs

White crane
standing in place

by the river this time
having travelled

many years to arrive
in this dry cold

light amidst the corn
making everything

possible the departing
the return what is

seen and what is not
still standing

      *

Flautist playing always
one note of the stone

stone fingers stopping
stone holes wind-played

starlit hunchbacked above
the timeless harmony

on one stone foot
sunlit dancing like any

stone skipping on water
while wholly at rest

beneath the clouds'
silent passage

    ...*

Hand pressing out
through blackened fire

five fingers reaching
through the uncounted

light of its seasons birds
stars clearly visible

in this place I stand
placing for a moment

my palm to this one
touching the start

    ...*

Bear sleeping
through stone winter

climbing now into sunlight
from the east shadow

of a mountain within which

others of your clan

astir now in stone grottos
leave dreams behind

turning to mewling cubs
who've slept thus far

their entire lives
only in stone

                    *

Serpentine series
ess curve proceeding

storyline traveling
millennia north to south

as does the river sinking
each winter underground

slip of a thing fragment
line of print squiggle

shining as does the river
in its telltale passing

Memory

Backstory
narrative structure

of things as they are
illuminating these goings-

on as the moon
illumines an earth

going round on its way
to this mythy place

dark silver milieu
a little owlet flies through

nostalgic for a whole
world she's never known

Balance

Nonjudgmental
thus capable of what is
as what is not

standing unmoved
between the rising and falling
bearing the load

to the center
of an earth always turning
its face thisaway

the scale pans
clanging like church bells
like fire bells

this *Belle Époque*
constant steadfast forever
swaying in the wind

Equinox

All things being equal
the day in its scales

rises apropos
its dark other

this first morning
of a season falling

backwards through
darkness through light

to the bare ground
it never once departs

on its long unmoving
return home

One

Space between
words say

not silence not
something else

making possible
everything that is

displacing that
which has no name

save the one said aloud
that we might tell

one another each time
the difference

Quotidian

When I came home I expected a surprise. There
was no surprise, so, of course, I was surprised.
                    Ludwig Wittgenstein

The appearance of nothing
out of the ordinary
startles us

the unworldly sky shifting
from lapis lazuli to
Kelly green

of an August day otherwise
unremarkable
as any

standing in the shadows
of itself waiting
to be seen

Vernal

Doubts don't produce leaves and branches
Dogen Kigen

Of this we're certain
as the mountain most certainly

ascends morning's blue rungs
rising though late snow

that was once cerulean sea
and will be again

because the great green-
eyed dragon stepping through

the garden gate upends
heaven and earth

and any last question
it is spring

Monument

Stone rings with the certitude of stone
and echoes in a firmament of arches

cast fire grew cold
still water darkened it

still it shown in the night
then stone was placed upon stone

flew into a tower and was crowned with a bell
or hung in the air over rivers

ephemeron old imperium
keystone securing the total vault

glister in the bezel of original position
the always coming before

Quintessence

In classical philosophy
the fifth and highest element

This one moves but obliquely
as light through a prism
made visible

first in its constituents
transpicuous as
they are

as our thinking must be
as the whole sky
that is

the same just-appreciable
blue we know
is not

there chalcedony flower
plainly visible
thin air

School Bus Yellow Sun Crayola Blue Sky

Some scenes are like this
scenes within a scene

waxwork standing in
for the earlier figure

light shining through
them both at once

then and now seen
clearly as any old thing

school bus yellow sun
the images it brings

down from on high
Crayola blue sky

Plot

Descending these stairs I'm
ascended by stairs
next steps on the long tramp
up from the acorn

through the moist dark
into the soft green
transparence breathing out
that we breathe in

to speak of through
the always-changing shapes
colors bright shouts
of the blue and redbirds

arc of the yellowhammer
eye of the woodsman
tooth of the saw
bouquet of the dust

hand of the carpenter
so on as so forth
traveling then as now
climbing helical

through so many stories
in all the tongues
without yet speaking
one of its own

Thus And So

No argument here
naught to augment the plaintext
fact of the matter

fine-grained as
maple wood as desert sand
blown this way

all the prints lead
through like words traveling
the undeclared

wilderness rising
about us unseen forest
for its trees

Case In Point

It's difficulty lies not in its being
abstruse silentious or occult

but in its being so

we begrudge it that
it's not what we had in mind

that aggregation of burrows and nests

we curl up in against
the dictates of fortune

the ravishments of time

all the variable monsters
bred in the bone

loose now on the open steppe

Commonsensical

Well of course you would
have to say and me too
as though such a thing were
not worth mention at all

a *porte cochère* one passes
quickly through en route
to the main event of a lifetime
lived out in that open

shared by the fields
the birds and the trees
in the unreflective view
of ordinary people

Kempt

Dark is the beauty of the brightest day
Christopher Marlowe

The robins are back each one
completely occupying his

or her roseate place in this whole
scheme of things wholly

inventive as the late snow
flurries this spring morning

the space between each fat
wet flake filled up with that

dark light the robins chirrup
the distances advance

the killings diminish not
in the least clearly visible now

as is middle night
bright with a splendor of its own

On The Contrary

The world weighs not
in a balance nor the time being
pass archival through

as sand an hourglass
nor is brown bat's eccentric
gallop on evening's air

any matter of course
any cursive *nom de guerre*
writ large that we

might read forever
at the once what is and thus
is not the case

Objet Trouvé

Out of everything
you are not
you came to be

as does the body
its day and the words
that say so

as does the silence
and the night overarching
shadow cast

by something else
that it is nonetheless
from the start

Acapulco Cliff Diver

for Hojosan

Seeing you niño midair
element in which you are

more at home than any other
moment caught like a breath

we feel your back arch
arms spread eyes meet ours

atop this sheer cliff face rising
from the grey-green surge

that began if such a thing can
be said ten thousand miles

straight out from here
returning now to the origin

of things salt displacing salt
because little angel you vanish

from sight and linger on
in this new element forever

Jumbo Et Alia

How high and white the morning clouds
ride piggyback the bluing sky

the humpback cumulous burly
bright company ascending that

last night's waning moon
made sad made sack

stubborn place comprised alack
of what's always right

before our eyes and quite
at hand and underfoot

there is ever this great space
but never between two things

Celestial Navigation

for Mom

Going on
by the light of our burning map

About the Author

Daniel Mintie is an adjunct professor at Georgetown University's School Of Medicine. The author of *Reclaiming Life After Trauma: Healing PTSD With Cognitive-Behavioral Therapy & Yoga; Dharma Wheels: Zen, Motorcycling & Cognitive-Behavioral Therapy;* and *My Tropic Of Cancer: Living & Dying With A Dread Disease*, he teaches at universities and training centers worldwide.

www.ingramcontent.com/pod-product-compliance
Lightning Source LLC
LaVergne TN
LVHW091224080426
835509LV00009B/1157